FINDING

5 Awakenings
to Your New Life

YOUR

WAY BACK

TO GOD

DAVE FERGUSON &
JON FERGUSON

MULTNOMAH
BOOKS

FINDING YOUR WAY BACK TO GOD PARTICIPANT'S GUIDE
PUBLISHED BY MULTNOMAH BOOKS
12265 Oracle Boulevard, Suite 200
Colorado Springs, Colorado 80921

Scripture quotations are taken from the Holy Bible, New International Version®, NIV®. Copyright © 1973, 1978, 1984, 2011 by Biblica Inc.™ Used by permission of Zondervan. All rights reserved worldwide. www.zondervan.com.

Trade Paperback ISBN 978-1-60142-673-4
eBook ISBN 978-1-60142-674-1

Cover design by Mark D. Ford

Published in the United States by WaterBrook Multnomah, an imprint of the Crown Publishing Group, a division of Penguin Random House LLC, New York.

MULTNOMAH and its mountain colophon are registered trademarks of Penguin Random House LLC.

Printed in the United States of America
2016

10 9 8 7 6

SPECIAL SALES
Most WaterBrook Multnomah books are available at special quantity discounts when purchased in bulk by corporations, organizations, and special-interest groups. Custom imprinting or excerpting can also be done to fit special needs. For information, please e-mail SpecialMarkets@WaterBrookMultnomah.com or call 1-800-603-7051.

CONTENTS

The Pathway

So many people today feel distant from God. Earlier in their lives they may have felt like they knew him. But then time passed, maybe something bad or disillusioning happened, and it was like they forgot him. Or he forgot them. Now they'd like to get back to God but aren't sure how.

I—Dave—know what that is like. So does my brother, Jon. We have both made and continue to make our own journeys back to God. We wrote the book *Finding Your Way Back to God* for spiritual searchers like ourselves.

How about you? Do you want to find your way back to God for the first time? Or maybe find your way back to him again?

If you are part of a Finding Your Way Back to God group, then you are on the right path. Your group will explore the key ideas from *Finding Your Way Back to God* as well as watch videos from the *Finding Your Way Back to God* DVD to discover the pathway God has laid out to lead people back to him.

This *Participant's Guide* is the tool to keep in your hands while you're searching for God alongside the other members of your group. Here you'll find all you need to participate fully in the five sessions.

Each session looks at one of the five awakenings that people typically have on their way back to God:

1. *An Awakening to Longing:* "There's got to be more."
2. *An Awakening to Regret:* "I wish I could start over."
3. *An Awakening to Help:* "I can't do this on my own."
4. *An Awakening to Love:* "God loves me deeply after all."
5. *An Awakening to Life:* "Now this is living!"

If you're not immediately sure of what all that means, no problem. That's what you'll discover in your group sessions. You'll see all five of these awakenings modeled in Jesus's story of the lost son (see Luke 15), giving you a map for how to find your way back to God.

I am certain that by the time you are done with the five sessions, you will be feeling connected to God once again. How can I be so confident? Because God wants to be found even more than we want to find him! Check out this promise from Jeremiah 29:12–14:

> "You will call on me and come and pray to me, and I
> will listen to you. You will seek me and find me when

you seek me with all your heart. I will be found by you,"
declares the LORD.

Now that gives us hope and reassurance, doesn't it? If we are
sincerely searching for God, we can have confidence because *he
is a findable God.*

So even if you're not sure God cares about you, even if
you're not clear on how to find your way back to him, even if
you're not totally convinced he really exists, what I'm asking
you to do is simply this: take a chance on him. Start by praying,
"God, if you are real, make yourself real to me." He will do it.
And he will use your Finding Your Way Back to God group as
a means of revealing himself to you.

You're on your way!

AWAKENING **TO** LONGING

"There's got to be more."

Session 1 Big Idea:

We all have a longing to love and be loved in return, to find purpose for our days, and to make sense out of life when life doesn't seem to make any sense. That longing is from God, and when you allow that strong desire for more to draw you nearer to him, he will fulfill your longings. God knows your needs and desires even better than you do, and he has a life of meaning and purpose in mind for you. The "more" you need most can only be found as you continually bring your life back to your heavenly Father. Let your longings for more—no matter how intense—draw you closer to him instead of pushing you away from him.

If possible, please read chapters 1–6 of *Finding Your Way Back to God* before participating in session 1.

OPTIONAL ICEBREAKER

Answer this question: What is one wild or rebellious act you committed as a teen or young adult that you now realize was foolish? (It doesn't have to be anything *too* embarrassing!)

OPENING THOUGHT AND DISCUSSION

1. Have you ever felt like you "lost" God somewhere along the course of your life (or perhaps never found him in the first place)? If so, describe the sense of separation you have felt and why you continue to want to find him.

2. What is your greatest longing? In other words, when you think of something you wish you had in your life but don't, or wish you understood about your life but can't, what is it?

Video Discussion

Watch video 1 on the *Finding Your Way Back to God* DVD, then discuss the following questions.

3. Think about Jake, Melissa, and Bryce, the three people in the video who told their stories of being far from God. Which one can you relate to the most, and why?

4. How do you feel about the wager that Jon Ferguson talks about in the video? Are you at a point in your life where you are prepared to pray, "God, if you are real, make yourself real to me"?

BIBLE DISCUSSION

Read Luke 15:11–32, the story of the lost son—the story we will be focusing on throughout this study.

> [11]There was a man who had two sons. [12]The younger one said to his father, "Father, give me my share of the estate." So he divided his property between them.
>
> [13]Not long after that, the younger son got together all he had, set off for a distant country and there squandered his wealth in wild living. [14]After he had spent everything, there was a severe famine in that whole country, and he began to be in need. [15]So he went and hired himself out to a citizen of that country, who

sent him to his fields to feed pigs. ¹⁶He longed to fill his stomach with the pods that the pigs were eating, but no one gave him anything.

¹⁷When he came to his senses, he said, "How many of my father's hired servants have food to spare, and here I am starving to death! ¹⁸I will set out and go back to my father and say to him: Father, I have sinned against heaven and against you. ¹⁹I am no longer worthy to be called your son; make me like one of your hired servants." ²⁰So he got up and went to his father.

But while he was still a long way off, his father saw him and was filled with compassion for him; he ran to his son, threw his arms around him and kissed him.

²¹The son said to him, "Father, I have sinned against heaven and against you. I am no longer worthy to be called your son."

²²But the father said to his servants, "Quick! Bring the best robe and put it on him. Put a ring on his finger and sandals on his feet. ²³Bring the fattened calf and kill it. Let's have a feast and celebrate. ²⁴For this son of mine was dead and is alive again; he was lost and is found." So they began to celebrate.

²⁵Meanwhile, the older son was in the field. When he came near the house, he heard music and dancing. ²⁶So he called one of the servants and asked him what was going on. ²⁷"Your brother has come," he replied,

"and your father has killed the fattened calf because he has him back safe and sound."

²⁸ The older brother became angry and refused to go in. So his father went out and pleaded with him. ²⁹ But he answered his father, "Look! All these years I've been slaving for you and never disobeyed your orders. Yet you never gave me even a young goat so I could celebrate with my friends. ³⁰ But when this son of yours who has squandered your property with prostitutes comes home, you kill the fattened calf for him!"

³¹ "My son," the father said, "you are always with me, and everything I have is yours. ³² But we had to celebrate and be glad, because this brother of yours was dead and is alive again; he was lost and is found."

5. Who do you think the three key figures in the story—the father and the two sons—represent?

6. When the younger son decided to ask for his inheritance and leave home, what do you think he was longing for?

LIFE APPLICATION DISCUSSION

7. *Finding Your Way Back to God* says that all of us have the feeling that "there's got to be more" to life. Specifically, there are at least three areas of life where all of us have legitimate longings: (a) to find love, (b) to find a purpose for life, and (c) to find meaning in our suffering. Describe a way in which you have a longing or desire in one of those three areas.

8. Have you ever had one of your major desires fulfilled but then found that the fulfillment wasn't enough—you were left with more longing and dissatisfaction? If so, describe the experience.

9. In what ways are your dissatisfactions and desires pushing you away from God? In what ways are they motivating you to seek God?

OPTIONAL PERSONAL DECISION TIME

Think back to the area of your life where you have the most acute sense of longing (identified in question 2). The next time you're feeling sad or dissatisfied about this lack in your life, use that emotion as a reminder to pray to God. Write down what, specifically, you want to say to God when you feel a sense of unsatisfied desire. Close your eyes now and pray the prayer. After you go home, begin to develop the habit of praying in response to your own feelings of dissatisfaction.

EXPANDED BIBLE DISCUSSION

Read John 4:4–26, the story of an encounter between Jesus and a woman at a well.

> [4][Jesus] had to go through Samaria. [5]So he came to a town in Samaria called Sychar, near the plot of ground Jacob had given to his son Joseph. [6]Jacob's well was there, and Jesus, tired as he was from the journey, sat down by the well. It was about noon.
>
> [7]When a Samaritan woman came to draw water, Jesus said to her, "Will you give me a drink?" [8](His disciples had gone into the town to buy food.)

⁹ The Samaritan woman said to him, "You are a Jew and I am a Samaritan woman. How can you ask me for a drink?" (For Jews do not associate with Samaritans.)

¹⁰ Jesus answered her, "If you knew the gift of God and who it is that asks you for a drink, you would have asked him and he would have given you living water."

¹¹ "Sir," the woman said, "you have nothing to draw with and the well is deep. Where can you get this living water? ¹² Are you greater than our father Jacob, who gave us the well and drank from it himself, as did also his sons and his livestock?"

¹³ Jesus answered, "Everyone who drinks this water will be thirsty again, ¹⁴ but whoever drinks the water I give them will never thirst. Indeed, the water I give them will become in them a spring of water welling up to eternal life."

¹⁵ The woman said to him, "Sir, give me this water so that I won't get thirsty and have to keep coming here to draw water."

¹⁶ He told her, "Go, call your husband and come back."

¹⁷ "I have no husband," she replied.

Jesus said to her, "You are right when you say you have no husband. ¹⁸ The fact is, you have had five husbands, and the man you now have is not your husband. What you have just said is quite true."

¹⁹ "Sir," the woman said, "I can see that you are a prophet. ²⁰ Our ancestors worshiped on this mountain, but you Jews claim that the place where we must worship is in Jerusalem."

²¹ "Woman," Jesus replied, "believe me, a time is coming when you will worship the Father neither on this mountain nor in Jerusalem. ²² You Samaritans worship what you do not know; we worship what we do know, for salvation is from the Jews. ²³ Yet a time is coming and has now come when the true worshipers will worship the Father in the Spirit and in truth, for they are the kind of worshipers the Father seeks. ²⁴ God is spirit, and his worshipers must worship in the Spirit and in truth."

²⁵ The woman said, "I know that Messiah" (called Christ) "is coming. When he comes, he will explain everything to us."

²⁶ Then Jesus declared, "I, the one speaking to you— I am he."

1. What longings do you think the woman had? How were these longings similar to the physical need for a drink to quench your thirst?

2. What is "living water"? How does it give permanent satisfaction?

Read Psalm 63:1–8, a poetic expression of David's great longing for, and confidence in, his God.

> [1] You, God, are my God,
>   earnestly I seek you;
> I thirst for you,
>   my whole being longs for you,
> in a dry and parched land
>   where there is no water.
>
> [2] I have seen you in the sanctuary
>   and beheld your power and your glory.
> [3] Because your love is better than life,
>   my lips will glorify you.
> [4] I will praise you as long as I live,
>   and in your name I will lift up my hands.
> [5] I will be fully satisfied as with the richest of foods;
>   with singing lips my mouth will praise you.

⁶ On my bed I remember you;

I think of you through the watches of the night.

⁷ Because you are my help,

I sing in the shadow of your wings.

⁸ I cling to you;

your right hand upholds me.

3. What images does David use to express his longing for God? Which one interests you the most, and why?

4. What indications do you see that God was able to satisfy David's longings?

Sometime after participating in session 1, find some quiet time to spend alone in a peaceful place with Scripture, your own thoughts, and prayer.

Read the following Scripture passage (Psalm 42:1–5):

¹As the deer pants for streams of water,
    so my soul pants for you, my God.
²My soul thirsts for God, for the living God.
    When can I go and meet with God?
³My tears have been my food day and night,
    while people say to me all day long,
        "Where is your God?"
⁴These things I remember
    as I pour out my soul:
how I used to go to the house of God
    under the protection of the Mighty One
with shouts of joy and praise
    among the festive throng.

⁵Why, my soul, are you downcast?
    Why so disturbed within me?
Put your hope in God,
    for I will yet praise him,
    my Savior and my God.

Underline one or more lines in the above passage that mean the most to you.

Think about these questions: *Lately, what have I been longing for? Is it possible that a longing for God is really at the root of all my other longings? Where is all this leading me?*

Pray the following prayer:

God, if you are real,
make yourself real to me.
Awaken in me the ability to see
that you are what's missing from my life.

Then go on to pray to God in your own words about your feeling that "there's got to be more."

AWAKENING TO REGRET

"I wish I could start over."

Session 2 Big Idea:

When we seek to fulfill our longings for love, purpose, and meaning on our own, we repeatedly find disappointment. The regret we feel for taking our own route can either lead to more longing and regret (we call it the "sorry cycle") or motivate us to seek help from the One who can help us most. You don't have to waste the power of your sincere regret on more self-condemnation and stuckness. You can let it move you confidently in God's direction. Why? Because now you know the truth, and it's a truth that you can put to work in your life over and over again in the years ahead: with God, we can *always* start over.

If possible, please read chapters 7 and 8 of *Finding Your Way Back to God* before participating in session 2.

OPTIONAL ICEBREAKER

Describe the following: (a) an item of clothing you're embarrassed to admit you used to wear, (b) a slang expression you can't believe you used to say, or (c) a singer or music group you're amazed that you used to like.

OPENING THOUGHT AND DISCUSSION

1. As you think back over the major decisions you've made in your life so far, what are some of your biggest regrets? How might these mistakes contribute to your feeling distant from God at times?

Video Discussion

Watch video 2 on the *Finding Your Way Back to God* DVD, then discuss the following questions.

2. How did you see a "sorry cycle" playing out in the lives of the people interviewed in the video?

3. Did Dave and Jon give you a different perspective on repentance than you've had before? If so, tell about that.

BIBLE DISCUSSION

Read Luke 15:11–19, showing how the son's choices brought him to a very different place from what he had sought.

[11] There was a man who had two sons. [12] The younger one said to his father, "Father, give me my share of the estate." So he divided his property between them.

[13] Not long after that, the younger son got together all he had, set off for a distant country and there squandered his wealth in wild living. [14] After he had spent everything, there was a severe famine in that whole country, and he began to be in need. [15] So he went and hired himself out to a citizen of that country, who sent him to his fields to feed pigs. [16] He longed to fill his stomach with the pods that the pigs were eating, but no one gave him anything.

[17] When he came to his senses, he said, "How many of my father's hired servants have food to spare, and here I am starving to death! [18] I will set out and go back to my father and say to him: Father, I have sinned against heaven and against you. [19] I am no longer worthy to be called your son; make me like one of your hired servants."

4. What regrets do you think the son felt when he was alone and had to toil at the lowest of low jobs just to stay alive?

5. How did his regrets lead him to attempt a "do-over" in his life?

6. By the time he made his decision to return home, how had his longings changed since the time when he had asked his dad for his inheritance?

LIFE APPLICATION DISCUSSION

7. Have you ever felt yourself stuck in a cycle of longing, disappointment, and regret? If so, describe what was going on.

8. How do you wish you could start over in your life? How do you think your life would be different if you could do it?

9. Do you feel you're ready now for a change that would bring you closer to God? If so, what's the next step?

If not, what's holding you back?

OPTIONAL PERSONAL DECISION TIME

Jesus assures us that "with God all things are possible" (Matthew 19:26). So no matter how many failures you may have had in the past, it's possible for you to have a fresh start in your life today. The starting point is to believe in the possibility. You have to say no to the cycle of longing, disappointment, and regret.

As best you can, define the way in which you need a new

start in your life by writing out the following sentences, filling in the blank:

I need to start over in my life by _____.

And I am confident that, with God's help, I can.

Pray for a fresh start.

EXPANDED BIBLE DISCUSSION

Read 2 Corinthians 7:8–10, where Paul analyzes how some early Christians had responded to his criticism.

> [8] Even if I caused you sorrow by my letter, I do not regret it. Though I did regret it—I see that my letter hurt you, but only for a little while— [9] yet now I am happy, not because you were made sorry, but because your sorrow led you to repentance. For you became sorrowful as God intended and so were not harmed in any way by us. [10] Godly sorrow brings repentance that leads to salvation and leaves no regret, but worldly sorrow brings death.

1. What would you say is the difference between "godly sorrow" and "worldly sorrow"?

2. What can you learn from this passage about how to use your regrets as a springboard for positive change in your life, rather than getting stuck in bitterness?

Read Isaiah 55:6–7, a passage that shows the clear connection between finding your way back to God and repenting of your errors.

> ⁶Seek the LORD while he may be found;
>   call on him while he is near.
> ⁷Let the wicked forsake their ways
>   and the unrighteous their thoughts.
> Let them turn to the LORD, and he will have
>   mercy on them,
>   and to our God, for he will freely pardon.

3. What encouragement do you find in these verses for people who have made bad choices?

Sometime after participating in session 2, find some quiet time to spend alone in a peaceful place with Scripture, your own thoughts, and prayer.

Read the following Scripture passage (Isaiah 43:16–21):

> [16] *This is what the LORD says—*
>   *he who made a way through the sea,*
>   *a path through the mighty waters,*
> [17] *who drew out the chariots and horses,*
>   *the army and reinforcements together,*
> *and they lay there, never to rise again,*
>   *extinguished, snuffed out like a wick:*
> [18] *"Forget the former things;*
>   *do not dwell on the past.*
> [19] *See, I am doing a new thing!*
>   *Now it springs up; do you not perceive it?*
> *I am making a way in the wilderness*
>   *and streams in the wasteland.*
> [20] *The wild animals honor me,*
>   *the jackals and the owls,*
> *because I provide water in the wilderness*
>   *and streams in the wasteland,*
> *to give drink to my people, my chosen,*

[21] *the people I formed for myself*
that they may proclaim my praise."

Underline one or more lines in the above passage that mean the most to you.

Think about these questions: *Where do I need a fresh start in my life? Am I ready to believe a fresh start is possible? What is God's role in all of this?*

Pray the following prayer:

> **God, if you are real,**
> **make yourself real to me.**
> **Awaken in me the possibility**
> **that with you I could start over again.**

Then continue your prayer time by talking to God about the need you feel to move past the place where you've gotten stuck and to begin again with him.

AWAKENING TO HELP

"I can't do this on my own."

Session 3 Big Idea:

Until we admit that we are powerless on our own to find fulfillment in this life, we will never truly find our way back to God.
But once we recognize our need for help, we have already made
the turn that leads us home to our heavenly Father. If you're like
every other person, you'll try to go it on your own many times
in the years to come. You'll even try to please and serve God on
your own—and that won't work either. You and I can't do it on
our own, and that is very good to know. Let your awakening to
your need for help continue to shape your choices in the years
ahead. Help has a name. His name is Jesus. And he will never
leave you. Every time you turn away from self-centeredness and
pride, he will be there to rescue, strengthen, and guide you on
your journey with him.

If possible, please read chapters 9–11 of *Finding Your Way
Back to God* before participating in session 3.

Optional Icebreaker

Share a funny story about a time when you got into a jam and needed help. This could be a story about your car getting stuck in the snow, getting a bracelet caught in your hair, or something like that.

Opening Thought and Discussion

1. Tell about a time when you tried to make a fresh start of some kind in your life—a new job, a new relationship, break a bad habit, or improve yourself—and failed. Looking back, why do you think it didn't work?

Video Discussion

Watch video 3 on the *Finding Your Way Back to God* DVD, then discuss the following questions.

2. How did Jeremy, Melissa, and J. R., interviewed in the video, experience their "I can't do this on my own" awakenings?

3. What was it in Dave and Jon's description of God that touched you the most, and why?

BIBLE DISCUSSION

Read Luke 15:14–20. This part of Jesus's story shows how the son humbled himself and went looking for the help he needed to start over again.

¹⁴After he had spent everything, there was a severe famine in that whole country, and he began to be in need. ¹⁵So he went and hired himself out to a citizen of that country, who sent him to his fields to feed pigs. ¹⁶He longed to fill his stomach with the pods that the pigs were eating, but no one gave him anything.

¹⁷When he came to his senses, he said, "How many of my father's hired servants have food to spare, and here I am starving to death! ¹⁸I will set out and go back to my father and say to him: Father, I have sinned against heaven and against you. ¹⁹I am no longer worthy to be called your son; make me like one of your hired servants." ²⁰So he got up and went to his father.

But while he was still a long way off, his father saw him and was filled with compassion for him; he ran to his son, threw his arms around him and kissed him.

4. When the son realized he needed some help, who did he think of, and why?

5. What kind of reaction did the young man expect from his father? What kind of reaction did he actually get?

6. What does the reaction by this father (representing God) teach you about having the confidence to return to God?

LIFE APPLICATION DISCUSSION

7. Would you say you are at a point of admitting you need help to lead a life different from the one you have? Why or why not?

8. What sort of response do you expect to receive from God if you come to him and ask him to accept you through grace?

OPTIONAL PERSONAL DECISION TIME

It's time to "come to your senses" and realize you need help to get out of the cycle of longing, disappointment, and regret. You don't have enough willpower to change on your own. Instead, you must surrender to the One who wants more for your life than you could ever imagine. Help has a name—*Jesus*.

Do one of two things:

(a) If you have never turned your life over to Jesus, do that now. In prayer, simply surrender to him, request forgiveness for your sins, and ask him to be your Leader forever.

OR

(b) If you are already a follower of Jesus, but have become estranged from him in some way, tell him that you want to re-commit your life to him. Ask for his help to put you back on the path of walking with him through life.

EXPANDED BIBLE DISCUSSION

Read Matthew 11:28–30, where Jesus issues an invitation to the "weary and burdened"—people for whom the life they have pursued on their own is proving harder and more disappointing than they anticipated.

> [28] Come to me, all you who are weary and burdened, and I will give you rest. [29] Take my yoke upon you and

learn from me, for I am gentle and humble in heart, and you will find rest for your souls. [30] For my yoke is easy and my burden is light.

1. How are the "weary and burdened" like the younger son in the parable? How are they like you?

2. What do these verses teach you about the kind of reception the needy get when they turn to God?

Read Romans 7:21–8:4. Here the apostle Paul talks about what finally cut through the knot of his spiritual frustration.

> [21] I find this law at work: Although I want to do good, evil is right there with me. [22] For in my inner being I delight in God's law; [23] but I see another law at work in me, waging war against the law of my mind and making me a prisoner of the law of sin at work within me. [24] What a wretched man I am! Who will rescue me from this body that is subject to death? [25] Thanks be to God, who delivers me through Jesus Christ our Lord!
>
> So then, I myself in my mind am a slave to God's law, but in my sinful nature a slave to the law of sin.
>
> [1] Therefore, there is now no condemnation for those who are in Christ Jesus, [2] because through Christ Jesus the law of the Spirit who gives life has set you free from the law of sin and death. [3] For what the law was powerless to do because it was weakened by the flesh, God did by sending his own Son in the likeness of sinful flesh to be a sin offering. And so he condemned sin in the flesh, [4] in order that the righteous requirement of the law might be fully met in us, who do not live according to the flesh but according to the Spirit.

3. What is Paul frustrated about in verses 21–24? How do you relate to this frustration?

4. Although Paul failed to earn the acceptance of the heavenly Father through trying hard to obey religious rules, what finally worked for him?

AFTER THE SESSION

Sometime after participating in session 3, find some quiet time to spend alone in a peaceful place with Scripture, your own thoughts, and prayer.

Read the following Scripture passage (John 3:16–21):

[16]God so loved the world that he gave his one and only Son, that whoever believes in him shall not perish but have eternal life. [17]For God did not send his Son into the world to condemn the world, but to save the world through him. [18]Whoever believes in him is not condemned, but whoever does not believe stands condemned already because they have not believed in the name of God's one and only Son. [19]This is the verdict: Light has come into the world, but people loved darkness instead of light because their deeds were evil. [20]Everyone who does evil hates the light, and will not come into the light for fear that their deeds will be exposed. [21]But whoever lives by the truth comes into the light, so that it may be seen plainly that what they have done has been done in the sight of God.

Underline one or more lines in the above passage that mean the most to you.

Think about these questions: *Why do I need a Savior to rescue me out of my separation from God? Am I at a place where I am ready to trust in Jesus, the Son of God, to bring me into the light of God's presence?*

Pray the following prayer:

> God, if you are real,
> make yourself real to me.
> Awaken in me the willingness
> to turn toward you for help.

As you continue to pray, tell God about your desires to move beyond the failures of your past and to begin a new life with him.

AWAKENING **TO** LOVE

"God loves me deeply after all."

Session 4 Big Idea:

We experience the irresistible love of God in Jesus when we finally return home to our Father. The grace he offers to every one of us is something we can't find anywhere else. It's almost shocking. It's overwhelming. It is continually amazing. And it is what we truly long for and were made to experience. As we awaken to God's love in our lives, some of the choices that seemed impossible before gradually become possible. Trusting God through the ups and downs of life becomes possible. Becoming more like his Son, Jesus Christ, becomes possible—and our deepest desire. And there's more: Believing in his faithful care for us and those we love makes absolute sense, infusing our days with God's peace. Knowing that not only does he love us but he loves everyone in the world just as deeply compels us to share the good news of Jesus with others. That's the wonder of

God's deep love for you and me. It has the power to heal us, change us, energize our hopes and dreams, and motivate us to serve him with our whole lives. So from this day forward, live boldly in his love. Never let doubt and discouragement take away what you know to be true!

If possible, please read chapters 12 and 13 of *Finding Your Way Back to God* before participating in session 4.

Optional Icebreaker

Tell about the first time you had a crush on someone. How did you express your feelings? How did the other person react?

Opening Thought and Discussion

1. Identify a time when you strongly felt the love of God toward you. What was your reaction?

VIDEO DISCUSSION

Watch video 4 on the *Finding Your Way Back to God* DVD, then discuss the following questions.

2. How did the people interviewed in the video struggle with doubt that God really loved them?

3. What did you learn from Dave and Jon about the new identity that the father in Jesus's parable gave to the son?

BIBLE DISCUSSION

Read Luke 15:20–24, the portion of Jesus's story where we observe the father's over-the-top expression of love for his son.

> [20] While [the son] was still a long way off, his father saw him and was filled with compassion for him; he ran to his son, threw his arms around him and kissed him.
>
> [21] The son said to him, "Father, I have sinned against heaven and against you. I am no longer worthy to be called your son."
>
> [22] But the father said to his servants, "Quick! Bring the best robe and put it on him. Put a ring on his finger and sandals on his feet. [23] Bring the fattened calf and kill it. Let's have a feast and celebrate. [24] For this son of mine was dead and is alive again; he was lost and is found." So they began to celebrate.

4. Identify as many different signs of the father's love as you can find in these verses.

5. What does the father's reaction toward his son tell you about God's attitude toward you when you repent and turn to him?

LIFE APPLICATION DISCUSSION

6. Tell about a way in which shame or guilt feelings have lingered in you even after you knew that you were forgiven and accepted by God. How has that leftover feeling of unworthiness affected your life?

7. If we have turned to God in repentance and received his acceptance, how can we help each other learn to accept our new identity as fully loved children of God?

8. Once we have accepted our identity as God's children, what are some ways in which our lives can be different and more fulfilling?

OPTIONAL PERSONAL DECISION TIME

No, you haven't earned God's love because you've performed so well in life or are such a great all-around person. But God offers his love to you anyway. It is a gift, boundless and free. May you never lose your wonder at God's love. And yet, may you learn to adjust your mind-set so that you can begin to live in the reality of the love that is yours.

Ask yourself these questions:

What are the kinds of situations that trigger your doubts about God's love for you?

When those situations arise, what Bible verse could you use to remind yourself of God's free gift of love to you? Write that verse here and decide that you will recall it whenever you need to hear God's voice of affirmation again.

EXPANDED BIBLE DISCUSSION

Read 1 John 3:1, a verse revealing that people have always needed some convincing that God's love is real—because it is so amazing.

> [1] See what great love the Father has lavished on us, that we should be called children of God! And that is what we are!

1. What do you think it is about becoming a child of God that is evidently so hard for people to accept?

Read Romans 8:31–39 on the invincible love of God toward us in Christ.

> [31] If God is for us, who can be against us? [32] He who did not spare his own Son, but gave him up for us all—how will he not also, along with him, graciously give us all things? [33] Who will bring any charge against those whom God has chosen? It is God who justifies. [34] Who

then is the one who condemns? No one. Christ Jesus who died—more than that, who was raised to life—is at the right hand of God and is also interceding for us. [35] Who shall separate us from the love of Christ? Shall trouble or hardship or persecution or famine or nakedness or danger or sword? [36] As it is written:

"For your sake we face death all day long;
    we are considered as sheep to be slaughtered."

[37] No, in all these things we are more than conquerors through him who loved us. [38] For I am convinced that neither death nor life, neither angels nor demons, neither the present nor the future, nor any powers, [39] neither height nor depth, nor anything else in all creation, will be able to separate us from the love of God that is in Christ Jesus our Lord.

2. Identify words or phrases from this passage revealing that God's love is *effective,* eliminating every last bit of condemnation. (See verses 31–34.)

3. Identify words or phrases from this passage revealing that God's love is *permanent,* resisting anything that might try to separate you from it. (See verses 35–39.)

4. How does God's effective and permanent love make you feel? How does his love give you confidence to trust him?

AFTER THE SESSION

Sometime after participating in session 4, find some quiet time to spend alone in a peaceful place with Scripture, your own thoughts, and prayer.

Read the following Scripture passage (Ephesians 3:14–19):

> [14] I kneel before the Father, [15] from whom every family in heaven and on earth derives its name. [16] I pray that out of his glorious riches he may strengthen you with power through his Spirit in your inner being, [17] so that Christ may dwell in your hearts through faith. And I pray that you, being rooted and established in love, [18] may have power, together with all the Lord's holy people, to grasp how wide and long and high and deep is the love of Christ, [19] and to know this love that surpasses knowledge—that you may be filled to the measure of all the fullness of God.

Underline one or more lines in the above passage that mean the most to you.

Think about these questions: *How can I learn to grasp the vast dimensions of God's love for me in Jesus? How can I learn not to take it for granted, but to accept it as real and to live in it?*

Pray the following prayer:

> God, if you are real,
> make yourself real to me.
> Awaken in me the awareness
> that I am your unconditionally loved child.

Thank God for his love, and ask him for the ability over time to gain a better sense of his love and a better sense of your identity in him by grace.

AWAKENING TO LIFE

"Now this is living!"

Session 5 Big Idea:

You know the way, and home is where you always belong. Be prepared in the years ahead for a life that's different from anything you thought possible when you made a U-turn on the road and asked the Father for help. The awakening to life brings with it unexpected influence and opportunities. How can this be? It's because Jesus is alive in you, and that changes just about everything. Now you can bring love to where there is hate. You can bring purpose to where there is confusion. You can bring hope to where there is despair. And that is living! So find your place in the community of other grateful sons and daughters of the Father. Connect with them, learn from them, and work alongside them to make a difference for good in homes, schools, workplaces, and communities. And together, let's keep helping others find their way back to God. That's where the real celebration is waiting.

If possible, please read chapters 14–16 of *Finding Your Way Back to God* before participating in session 5.

OPTIONAL ICEBREAKER

Share your answer to this question: When do you feel most alive?

OPENING THOUGHT AND DISCUSSION

1. What changes have you already seen in yourself during the process of returning to God? What changes do you hope to see for yourself in your future?

VIDEO DISCUSSION

Watch video 5 on the *Finding Your Way Back to God* DVD, then discuss the following questions.

2. Would you say that you have a zoe kind of life? If so, describe it.

3. What was it in the video that most inspired you about living joyfully in the knowledge of God's acceptance of you?

BIBLE DISCUSSION

Read Luke 15:22–24. You've already read these verses, but this time focus on the reason in verse 24 that the father gives for the celebration. (Also see verse 32.)

> 22 The father said to his servants, "Quick! Bring the best robe and put it on him. Put a ring on his finger and sandals on his feet. 23 Bring the fattened calf and kill it. Let's have a feast and celebrate. 24 For this son of mine was dead and is alive again; he was lost and is found." So they began to celebrate.

4. In what sense was the son "dead" and "lost"? In what sense is he now "alive" and "found"?

5. Would you say that the same dramatic contrasts (alive after being dead, found after being lost) are appropriate to describe the changes in us when we find our way back to God? Give your reasons.

Life Application Discussion

6. Do you worship regularly as part of a church family? If so, describe the worship at your church. How does it help to sustain you in your new life with God?

If not, what might it take for you to find a church and consistently join in the worship?

7. Do you have a regular devotional time of Bible reading, reflection, and prayer? If so, describe your private devotional practice. How does it help to sustain you in your new life with God?

If not, how could you begin to make this a habit in your life?

8. Are you part of a small group of people who want to live in the love of God and meet together regularly? If so, tell about your small group and how it functions. How does it help to sustain you in your new life with God?

If not, how could you find a small group that fits your needs during this season of your life?

9. Do you engage in some kind of ministry or service
   (however informal) that seeks to bless others? If so, explain
   this ministry. How does it help to sustain you in your new
   life with God?

If not, what kind of ministry do you think God has equipped
you to be involved with in order to bring his blessing into the
lives of others?

OPTIONAL PERSONAL DECISION TIME

Think back to your answers to questions 6–9. These questions get at four key practical ways in which you can live out your new life in Christ: public worship, private devotions, small-group participation, and personal ministry. Choose at least one area where you know you are not doing what you could, then settle on at least one specific step you will take to live out your new spiritual identity. (For example, if you are not in a small group but would like to be, then maybe this week you could contact the leader who coordinates small groups in your church.) Write down what you plan to do.

Remember, Jesus says, "I am making everything new!" (Revelation 21:5).

EXPANDED BIBLE DISCUSSION

Read John 3:1–8, the account of a time when Jesus mystified a religious teacher by talking about being "born again."

[1] Now there was a Pharisee, a man named Nicodemus who was a member of the Jewish ruling council. [2] He came to Jesus at night and said, "Rabbi, we know that you are a teacher who has come from God. For no one could perform the signs you are doing if God were not with him."

[3] Jesus replied, "Very truly I tell you, no one can see the kingdom of God unless they are born again."

[4] "How can someone be born when they are old?" Nicodemus asked. "Surely they cannot enter a second time into their mother's womb to be born!"

[5] Jesus answered, "Very truly I tell you, no one can enter the kingdom of God unless they are born of water and the Spirit. [6] Flesh gives birth to flesh, but the Spirit gives birth to spirit. [7] You should not be surprised at my saying, 'You must be born again.' [8] The wind blows wherever it pleases. You hear its sound, but you cannot tell where it comes from or where it is going. So it is with everyone born of the Spirit."

1. What do you think Jesus was trying to get Nicodemus to understand?

2. What does this passage teach you about how God is working in a spiritual and unseen manner within you while you're trying to move toward him?

Read 2 Corinthians 5:16–18 and Romans 6:3–4, where Paul echoes other biblical teaching on the "new life." (Also see Isaiah 65:17–25 and Revelation 21:1–22:5.)

¹⁶ From now on we regard no one from a worldly point of view. Though we once regarded Christ in this way,

we do so no longer. ¹⁷ Therefore, if anyone is in Christ, the new creation has come: The old has gone, the new is here! ¹⁸ All this is from God, who reconciled us to himself through Christ. (2 Corinthians 5:16–18)

³ Or don't you know that all of us who were baptized into Christ Jesus were baptized into his death? ⁴ We were therefore buried with him through baptism into death in order that, just as Christ was raised from the dead through the glory of the Father, we too may live a new life. (Romans 6:3–4)

3. What do you think is included in the newness that comes to people who are reconciled to God through Christ?

4. How does baptism represent this new life in Christ?

Sometime after participating in session 5, find some quiet time to spend alone in a peaceful place with Scripture, your own thoughts, and prayer.

Read the following Scripture passage (Colossians 3:1–4):

[1] Since . . . you have been raised with Christ, set your hearts on things above, where Christ is, seated at the right hand of God. [2] Set your minds on things above, not on earthly things. [3] For you died, and your life is now hidden with Christ in God. [4] When Christ, who is your life, appears, then you also will appear with him in glory.

Underline one or more lines in the above passage that mean the most to you.

Think about these questions: *How has my life changed since coming back to God? What can I do to get rid of the remnants of my old life and live in a way that's more consistent with my new life?*

Pray the following prayer:

> **God, if you are real,**
> **make yourself real to me.**
> **Awaken in me the confidence**
> **that I can live a brand-new life.**

Thank the Lord for drawing you near when you felt separated from him. Ask his help to remain close to him for your whole life long—and throughout all eternity!

Leader's Guide

A *Finding Your Way Back to God* group isn't a formal class, and it doesn't require a trained teacher. Still, it is helpful to have someone who will organize the experience and facilitate the discussions—in other words, an informal leader of the group.

Could that be you? If so, thanks for your investment in the lives of people trying to find their way back to God!

In the pages that follow, this "Leader's Guide" section of the book will give you specific guidance for each of the five sessions. Before we get to that, however, let's look at some tips you may want to use before the first session.

- *Advertise the group.* Personally invite people and get the word out about the group. You may want to do this through your local church or through posting a notice at a local café or club or perhaps through social media.

- *Get organized.* Order copies of this book for all
  the participants as well as a copy of the *Finding
  Your Way Back to God* DVD. Gather the names,
  phone numbers, and e-mail addresses of people
  who are planning to participate so that you can
  send them reminders. Select a meeting place.
  Make sure you have a television with a DVD
  player available. Arrange for refreshments.
- *Prepare yourself.* Be in prayer for yourself and the
  other people in the group. Read each session, along
  with the corresponding chapters of *Finding Your
  Way Back to God,* before the session time. Have
  some of your own stories and thoughts ready to
  share.

Above all, welcome people to the group with the same kind
of love and acceptance that God has for spiritual wanderers!

Awakening to Longing

Objective: To help participants discover that their longings are from God and that, when they allow those strong desires to draw them nearer to him, he will fulfill their longings.

What you need for this session:

- At least one copy of the book *Finding Your Way Back to God* to refer to if needed
- The *Finding Your Way Back to God* DVD
- A DVD player and a screen on which the whole group can watch video 1
- Bibles for yourself and the other participants
- (optional) Index cards or slips of paper
- (optional) Pens or pencils

OPTIONAL ICEBREAKER

Welcome the members of the group to the first session. You may choose to set a friendly tone by getting the group members discussing the icebreaker question.

OPENING THOUGHT AND DISCUSSION

Questions 1 and 2: These questions are rather personal, so don't push any of the group members to respond to them verbally. Instead, ask for one or two volunteers to share their responses to each question. If the other group members only want to think about their answers on their own, that's fine.

VIDEO DISCUSSION

Questions 3 and 4: After playing the video, use these questions to help group members react to what they saw.

BIBLE DISCUSSION

Questions 5 and 6: Use these questions first to give the group members an overview of the parable of the lost son and then to focus on how the younger son had misguided longings that led him to "a distant country."

LIFE APPLICATION DISCUSSION

Questions 7 to 9: If some group members are hesitant to say too much about the unfulfilled longings in their life, that's okay. If some express bitterness or sorrow, that's okay too. Let people be real about their feelings. Yet to the extent that you can, help the others begin to see what it looks like in the lives of everyday people when they start turning to God for the love, purpose, and meaning they lack in life. If you have a large group, you may want to split it into two or more smaller groups so that everyone who has a desire to speak up about his or her own story can do so.

OPTIONAL
PERSONAL DECISION TIME

Use this as a concluding activity if you have time and want the group members to make a personal response to the discussion you've been having.

Hand out index cards or slips of paper, plus pens or pencils, to the group members. You might want to invite the group members to scatter to different spots in your meeting area for quiet, individual reflection while they decide what to write. After a few minutes, gather them again and ask for a volunteer or two to share what they wrote down.

EXPANDED BIBLE DISCUSSION

If you have time in the session to discuss more of the Bible, use one or both of the passages in this expanded material. (You may wish to insert these questions following the discussion of Luke 15:11–32 in questions 5 and 6 above.)

Expanded questions 1 and 2: Make sure the group members recognize that the story of the woman at the well shows how a person's longing for love can help to draw her or him toward God's love. The same is true for other kinds of longings.

Expanded questions 3 and 4: Some of the group members may share David's intense yearning for God. Others might wish they did but aren't there yet. At this point, just help them all to get a glimpse of what longing for God can look like.

CLOSING PRAYER

Lead in prayer, asking God to help everyone in the group convert his or her longings for "more" into a pursuit of God's greater presence in their life.

PREVIEW OF THE NEXT SESSION

Whet the group members' appetites for session 2 by telling them it has the encouraging message that *everyone* can start over again!

Awakening to Regret

Objective: To help participants realize that they don't have to waste regret on more self-condemnation and stuckness but can let their regret move them in God's direction.

What you need for this session:

- At least one copy of the book *Finding Your Way Back to God* to refer to if needed
- The *Finding Your Way Back to God* DVD
- A DVD player and a screen on which the whole group can watch video 2
- Bibles for yourself and the other participants
- (optional) Index cards or slips of paper
- (optional) Pens or pencils

Optional Icebreaker

If you choose to use this session's icebreaker, share your own examples of an embarrassing item of clothing, slang expression, or music group you used to think was cool but now are embarrassed by.

Opening Thought and Discussion

Question 1: This question may open up wounds for some group members, so don't force anyone to respond verbally. But model openness by sharing your own response.

Video Discussion

Questions 2 and 3: After playing the video, use these questions to help group members react to what they saw.

Bible Discussion

Questions 4 to 6: Help your fellow group members see how the opening verses of the lost son story illustrate this session's theme: The son had a longing for freedom and fun, but instead of his actions leading him to happiness, they led to misery. Yet to his credit, rather than just feeling sorry for himself in his humiliating job, he chose to start over.

LIFE APPLICATION DISCUSSION

Questions 7 to 9: Help group members wrestle with their need to start over if they are going to have their deepest longings fulfilled and find their way back to God. Some may readily accept the message of starting afresh. Others might feel hopeless. Be sympathetic and encouraging.

OPTIONAL PERSONAL DECISION TIME

Use this as a concluding activity if you have time and want the group members to make a personal response to the discussion you've been having.

Hand out index cards or slips of paper, plus pens or pencils, to the group members. Then invite the group members to scatter to different spots in your meeting area for quiet reflection while they decide how to complete their sentence. Encourage them to take a few moments for individual prayer before you gather the group together again.

EXPANDED BIBLE DISCUSSION

If you have time in the session to discuss more of the Bible, use one or both of the passages in this expanded material. (You may wish to insert these questions following the discussion of Luke 15:11–19 in questions 4 and 5 above.)

Expanded questions 1 and 2: Before the session starts, read all of 2 Corinthians 7 so that you are familiar with the context for the quoted verses. The key point to note is that remorse and regret can be poisonous if we don't move beyond them, but they can be life-giving if they lead to repentance and change.

Expanded question 3: In introducing this inspiring quote from Isaiah, remind the group of the definition of *repentance* found in chapter 8 of *Finding Your Way Back to God*. Repentance is "a turning point. It means to turn from whatever is distracting you or pulling you away from God and to intentionally turn toward God."

CLOSING PRAYER

If you sense that one particular member of the group is especially excited about the idea of getting unstuck and starting over, invite him or her to close the session with prayer, asking God to give each group member hope for positive change.

PREVIEW OF THE NEXT SESSION

Tell your fellow group members that there is one little problem with coming to a realization that you need to start over: *you can't start over on your own!* They should come back next time for the solution to this problem.

Awakening to Help

Objective: To help participants realize they need to admit they are powerless on their own to find fulfillment in life, and they need to go to Jesus for help.

What you need for this session:

- At least one copy of the book *Finding Your Way Back to God* to refer to if needed
- The *Finding Your Way Back to God* DVD
- A DVD player and a screen on which the whole group can watch video 3
- Bibles for yourself and the other participants

OPTIONAL ICEBREAKER

If you choose to use this week's icebreaker, let the participants know that the theme of this session is the need for help.

OPENING THOUGHT AND DISCUSSION

Question 1: Some group members may want to talk about fairly inconsequential attempts to make a fresh start, such as losing weight by going on a diet. That's okay. But try to elicit at least one example of a more serious need to start over in life, such as moving past an addiction or recovering from a divorce.

VIDEO DISCUSSION

Questions 2 and 3: After playing the video, use these questions to help group members react to what they saw.

BIBLE DISCUSSION

Questions 4 to 6: The son recognized that he needed help, and so he went home to his father. Likewise, we must turn to God when we need a fresh start in life. And just as the father in the story was immediately welcoming to the son, so we can trust that God will receive us with open arms when we return to him.

LIFE APPLICATION
DISCUSSION

Questions 7 and 8: Try to help the group members be honest with themselves about their need for help from God. After all, the awakening to help is *the* turning point on the path back to God! Either your fellow group members will pass successfully through this turning point and find their way to the Father who loves them, or they will turn back into useless regret and disappointment.

OPTIONAL
PERSONAL DECISION TIME

Use this as a concluding activity if you have time and want the group members to make a personal response to the discussion you've been having.

Invite the group members to scatter to different spots in your meeting area to do business with God individually. If you believe that some members of the group need to put their faith in Jesus for the first time, offer to pray with them. Or pair them with other mature followers of Christ. Encourage all others to recommit themselves to following Jesus. Offer to provide further help and guidance after the session to anyone who might want it.

EXPANDED BIBLE DISCUSSION

If you have time in the session to discuss more of the Bible, use one or both of the passages in this expanded material. (You may wish to insert these questions following the discussion of Luke 15:17–20 in questions 4 to 6 above.)

Expanded questions 1 and 2: Help the group members see themselves as those who are "weary and burdened" with regrets. Jesus calls us to him and is eager to lift our burdens from us.

Expanded questions 3 and 4: The theology here is pretty heavy, so you may want to get out your Bible and read the context surrounding the quoted verses. But the key point is straightforward: As much as we may try to do what's right in our own strength, we are ultimately incapable of acting in a way that's perfectly correct. Yet we are not hopelessly trapped in condemnation because of our failure. We can be freed by the grace available in Christ. Thanks be to God!

CLOSING PRAYER

Invite group members to contribute prayers of thanks and praise to God for providing help for us through his Son, Jesus.

PREVIEW OF THE NEXT SESSION

Tell the group members something like this: "God loves us! That's so amazing that it can be hard for us to accept. So session 4 is all about learning to live out our new identity as God's beloved sons and daughters."

Awakening to Love

Objective: To help participants choose to live boldly in God's love, never letting doubt and discouragement take away what they know to be true.

What you need for this session:

- At least one copy of the book *Finding Your Way Back to God* to refer to if needed
- The *Finding Your Way Back to God* DVD
- A DVD player and a screen on which the whole group can watch video 4
- Bibles for yourself and the other participants
- (optional) Index cards or slips of paper
- (optional) Pens or pencils

- (optional) A Bible concordance or similar Bible reference tool

OPTIONAL ICEBREAKER

You may wish to use this icebreaker to warm up the group for the session. Try to keep the discussion from embarrassing anyone. Keep the conversation light.

OPENING THOUGHT AND DISCUSSION

Question 1: Hopefully, in response to this question, you will get some stories in which participants testify to how they felt overwhelmed by God's love. If not, tell a story from your own life in which you could hardly believe it was true that God loved you so much.

VIDEO DISCUSSION

Questions 2 and 3: After playing the video, use these questions to help group members react to what they saw.

BIBLE DISCUSSION

Questions 4 and 5: If you want to expand on the meaning of the robe, the ring, and the sandals, see chapter 13 of *Finding*

Your Way Back to God. The key point is that, just as the father in the story shared his own identity with his son, so God shares his identity with us. In other words, when we return to him, we belong to him and we share in his blessings.

LIFE APPLICATION DISCUSSION

Questions 6 to 8: The message of this session is simple: "You are loved. So live like it!" In this life application discussion, help group members move toward acceptance of their new identity as beloved sons and daughters of the heavenly Father.

OPTIONAL PERSONAL DECISION TIME

Use this as a concluding activity if you have time and want the group members to make a personal response to the discussion you've been having.

Hand out index cards or slips of paper, along with pencils or pens, for participants to write the Bible verse each has chosen. Invite the group members to scatter to different spots in your meeting area for personal reflection on the verses they want to use to help them live in—and live out of—God's love. Meanwhile, you may wish to have a Bible reference tool such as a concordance on hand to help group members identify a verse to memorize. (You could also have a computer logged on to an online Bible search tool.) If nothing else, group members may want to use 1 John 3:1: "See what great love the Father has lavished on us, that we should be called children of God! And that is what we are!"

Just as Jesus used the Word of God to help him fight back against the devil's temptations (see Matthew 4:1–11), so you and your fellow group members can use Scripture promises to help you avoid the temptation to reject or downplay the love of God toward you.

EXPANDED BIBLE DISCUSSION

If you have time in the session to discuss more of the Bible, use one or both of the passages in this expanded material. (You may wish to insert these questions following the discussion of Luke 15:20–24 in questions 4 and 5 above.)

Expanded question 1: Deep down, we all know that we are sinners who have done nothing to earn God's grace. Adoption as his child is a continual wonder!

Expanded questions 2 to 4: Your group members may have been disappointed before by people loving them but eventually taking that love away. Help them to see that God's love is different. It transforms us and, through faith in Christ, is ours forever.

CLOSING PRAYER

Lead in prayer, praising God for his overwhelming love and asking him to help all the group members live in his love, with gratitude and boldness, from this day forward.

PREVIEW OF THE NEXT SESSION

Encourage the group members to be present for the final session, and tell them that it will give them practical ways to live out their new life as children of God.

Awakening to Life

Objective: To help participants celebrate their new life by finding their place in the community of grateful sons and daughters of the Father.

What you need for this session:

- At least one copy of the book *Finding Your Way Back to God* to refer to if needed
- The *Finding Your Way Back to God* DVD
- A DVD player and a screen on which the whole group can watch video 5
- Bibles for yourself and the other participants
- (optional) Index cards or slips of paper
- (optional) Pens or pencils
- (optional) Information group members can

use to begin corporate and personal worship, small-group participation, and service to others in your community

OPTIONAL ICEBREAKER

If you decide to use this icebreaker question with your group, examples of answers might include playing extreme sports, traveling to exotic locales, and performing with a musical instrument.

OPENING THOUGHT AND DISCUSSION

Question 1: Be as affirming as you can about the positive changes taking place in group members' lives. Give God the credit for it all.

VIDEO DISCUSSION

Questions 2 and 3: After playing the video, use these questions to help group members react to what they saw.

BIBLE DISCUSSION

Questions 4 and 5: The Scriptures frequently use dramatic contrasts, such as death and life (see Ephesians 2:1–10; Colossians

2:9–15), to talk about the difference between not knowing God and knowing him. Help your fellow group members see that finding one's way back to God is not just an *improvement* to someone's life—it is a *new* life.

LIFE APPLICATION DISCUSSION

Questions 6 to 9: If your group is large, you may wish to break it into small groups so that everyone has time to discuss these application questions. Don't make anyone feel guilty for not going to church regularly or otherwise failing to do these things he or she "should" be doing. Instead, help group members see that worship, devotions, small groups, and service are means that God has provided to help us maintain a growing relationship with him. They do not need to be a duty but a joy!

OPTIONAL PERSONAL DECISION TIME

Use this as a concluding activity if you have time and want the group members to make a personal response to the discussion you've been having.

Hand out index cards or slips of paper, along with pencils or pens, for participants to write their decisions down. Then invite the group members to go to different spots in your meeting area in groups of two or three to discuss their decisions.

If possible, be prepared with practical information people

can use. Maybe you could have a few examples of devotional guides you like. Or maybe you can have the contact information people can use to get in touch with leaders in your church about joining a small group or participating with a ministry team.

EXPANDED BIBLE DISCUSSION

If you have time in the session to discuss more of the Bible, use one or both of the passages in this expanded material. (You may wish to insert these questions following the discussion of Luke 15:22–24 in questions 4 and 5 above.)

Expanded questions 1 and 2: "Born again" is another way to talk about having new life. This passage gives a glimpse into the mysterious yet powerful way in which the Spirit of God is at work behind the scenes as we are seeking to find our way back to God.

Expanded question 3: Group members may refer to such things as peace, joy, holiness, purpose, and assurance of an eternity with God. All such are true.

CLOSING PRAYER

Invite volunteers to express their feelings to God about drawing near to him as lost sons and daughters who have now been found.

God, if you're real, make yourself real to me.

Discover the core book behind the study. Get on the road of authentic spiritual discovery—starting where you are. Then, go even deeper by taking the next step with the 5-part *Finding Your Way Back to God DVD*. In each 10-minute session, Dave and Jon guide you through a life awakening, inspiring you to follow the path God has laid out for returning to Him.

Find additional resources to further your study at BigIdeaResources.com/fywbtg